Globalization and War

——

The Aftermath

WORKS BY MALAQUIAS MONTOYA

An exhibition organized by the
Office of the Vice Chancellor of Student Affairs at the University of California, Irvine

La violencia institucionalizada, la miseria y la opresión generan una realidad dual, fruto de la persistencia de sistemas políticos y económicos creadores de injusticias, que consagran un orden social que beneficia a unos pocos: ricos cada vez más ricos a costa de pobres cada vez más pobres.[1]

Adolfo Pérez Esquivel

Nobel Peace Prize Recipient, 1980

The institutionalized violence, misery and

oppression generate a dual reality, fruit of the

political and economic systems that create

injustice, sanctifying a social order that benefits

only a few: the rich become ever richer at the

expense of the poor who become ever poorer.[2]

Adolfo Pérez Esquivel

Nobel Peace Prize Recipient, 1980

Acknowledgments

Malaquias Montoya and Lezlie Salkowitz-Montoya gratefully acknowledge the generous contributions toward the publication of this catalogue. Major support has been provided by:

Office of the Vice Chancellor
Manuel Gomez
University of California, Irvine

Institute for Latino Studies
Dr. Gilberto Cardenas, Director
Assistant Provost & Director
University of Notre Dame

Chicana/o Studies Program
Dr. Adela de la Torre, Director
University of California, Davis

The LEF Foundation

Quinn Delaney
Oakland, CA

El Centro Chicano
Dr. Frances Morales
Associate Dean & Director
Stanford University

Latino/a Studies
Dr. Jose David, Director
Jenny Snead Williams
Duke University

Additional heartfelt thanks to other contributors: Ricardo & Harriet Romo, *San Antonio, Texas*; Dr. José Limón & Dolores Garcia, CEMAS, *University of Texas @ Austin*; Chon Noriega, CSRC, *University of California, Los Angeles* and Dr. Emily Prieto, LRC, *Northern Illinois University.*

Special Thanks to Jesús Barraza, Layout & Design
Dr. Joanna Miller & Maceo Montoya, Editors

Photography & Research: Lezlie Salkowitz-Montoya

Co-published by Malaquias Montoya and Lezlie Salkowitz-Montoya, and the Institute for Latino Studies, University of Notre Dame.

For ordering information contact:
Lezlie Salkowitz-Montoya, Post Office Box 6, Elmira, CA 95625
lsmontoya@earthlink.net
www.malaquiasmontoya.com

Cover image: *Globalization*, 2005, Acrylic Painting, 64x52 inches

ISBN# 978-0-615-20316-4
Printed in the United Sates of North America
InkWorks Press
www.inkworkspress.org

Introduction

Malaquias Montoya: The Beating Heart of a Chicano Artist

Why do we kill and what happens to us as human beings?
How does the victim obtain justice?

These two questions, which Malaquias Montoya asked in an essay on capital punishment,[3] are clearly still on his mind. All one has to do is look through his latest works in this collection, *Globalization & War: The Aftermath*, (the inaugural exhibit was held at the University of California, Irvine in November, 2007) to see how well Malaquias understands the complex relationship between victim and victimizer. The way he brings together immigration, terrorism, American imperialism, torture, and other themes related to America's global presence and influence invites us to see past our own comfortable positions as bystanders, bringing us more directly into the full horror and traumatic realities of globalization and war.

I have known Malaquias for many years; in fact, my profile appears on one of the political posters he was creating during his early years as an artist-activist in the Chicano Movement.* Even then Malaquias was drawing parallels between what was happening at home and abroad. He understood that some of the same forces that oppressed Chicanos, African Americans, American Indians, and women in the United States were also mani-

He has asked over and over again, how violence can be justified in a democratic state, and his work conveys how devastating the effects of national, political, and cultural arrogance can be

fest in the American involvement in Vietnam. Early on Malaquias Montoya distinguished himself as an artist who took an active stand against the continued persecution of the voiceless and the invisible –victims we fail to see in the midst of our own political and cultural justifications.

Although Malaquias has evolved and grown as an artist, his central vision and voice have remained consistently trained on giving us an intimate understanding of how little can separate so-called justice from victimization. He has asked over and over again, how violence can be justified in a democratic state, and his work conveys how devastating the effects of national, political, and cultural arrogance can be.

The images in this collection are disturbing, necessarily so. From the contorted faces of torture victims to the disfigured bodies of ordinary citizens, Malaquias counts the very human cost of democracy where it spreads, not like a protective cloak, but rather like a pernicious virus, armed with land mines and instruments of torture and religious and ethnic intolerance. In the mirror he holds up to our nation's global presence, we see ourselves as no better than the dogs who tear at the bodies of those we declare enemies, but who are, in reality, human beings as we are, victims of what has been proclaimed a just, even holy, war. We are provoked to think again about those who seek our borders for asylum, for the promise of a better life Americans so proudly espouse.

The images in this collection incite, provoke, argue, plead, and accuse, asking us over and over, "Who is the victim here?" and "Where is the justice here?" And whether the "here" is the United States or Iraq or Afghanistan or Vietnam or Mexico, the questions remain largely the same. As Malaquias unflinchingly reminds us over and over again, we are all human beings, and ultimately it is our own humanity on trial. What will the verdict be? That, Malaquias Montoya suggests, depends on our willingness to see justice as a universal human condition, and not the property of one country or culture. He refuses to surrender his suffering heart.

He paints and fights against the delusions and terrorism of war and its aftermath. His paintings are not abstract nor are they silent. His

*Mexican American Liberation Art Front
1969, Silkscreen

work is an invitation to open our eyes and see ourselves and others -- anew. Indeed, his work speaks to the ultimate triumph of the human spirit.

Manuel N. Gomez
Vice Chancellor,
University of California, Irvine
February 11, 2008

6

Globalization & War – The Aftermath

by Malaquias Montoya

Socio-political narrative has always been an important part of my work. My emphasis on content is a departure from the formalist orientation of most artists who concern themselves with visual abstraction and find delight with the play of color and shape, and the spatial relationships of these elements. This self-concerned ideology has dominated the art world for the past century, and, as a result, any artist that breaks away from this tradition is viewed questionably. My images are intended to confront the multitude of socially disengaging and crippling images given to us by our daily media, images that disguise reality, manipulate consciousness, and lull the creative imagination to sleep. My artwork celebrates the small and large victories of the human spirit and pays tribute to those who struggle and suffer the consequences of those in power.

This work presents a mirror for viewers to see themselves in portraits that focus on the human spirit at its most vulnerable, in the shadows between obliteration, devastation, and survival.

The current exhibition began to develop in 2002-03 when I started seriously investigating and exploring issues of migration. My research resulted in a series of paintings. This body of work soon developed into an examination of people displaced as a result of global capitalism. At the same time, I was also deeply affected by the horrors of the reports on the torture that took place at Abu Ghraib and Guantánamo Bay. It was then, that I began producing a series of silkscreen prints, paintings, and other works on paper depicting the dreadfulness of the horrendous acts imposed by our government.

Globalization & War – The Aftermath attempts to illuminate the inhumanity of the unspeakable acts of war, and corporate globalization, and their resulting displacement. Globalization is another form of colonization, and war is both its vehicle and its consequence. Who benefits? Certainly not those whose homes and cities have been destroyed, or those who return maimed in body and soul. In a quote that remains relevant today, USMC Major General Smedley D. Butler, a two-time Congressional Medal of Honor Recipient from WWI, states:

War is a racket....best described as something that is not what it seems to the majority of people. Only a small "inside" group knows what it is about. It is conducted for the benefit of the very few, at the expense of the very many...It is the only one international in scope. It is the only one in which the profits are reckoned in dollars and the losses in lives.[4]

It is an honor for me as an artist to produce artwork that is socially and politically aware, but the most rewarding aspect of this project will be the response and dialogue that I hope this work encourages. My work is an art of partisanship, an art that stirs feelings and calls for the viewer to take sides in a very personal way. To name just a few, Jose Clemente Orozco, David Alfaro Siqueros,

Elizabeth Catlett, and Kathe Kollwitz, all have participated in creating this type of overpowering artistic document, each charged with the utmost personal commitment to humanity.

My work is often referred to as propaganda art. I don't mind being labeled as such since I feel all work is propagandist in nature; it just depends whom you want to propagandize for. From cave painting to the present, art has always spoken on someone's behalf.

With this exhibition I hope to convey the consequences of power and war, a universal story that involves peoples of all cultures and nationalities. This work presents a mirror for viewers to see themselves in portraits that focus on the human spirit at its most vulnerable, in the shadows between obliteration, devastation, and survival. My hope is that the viewer is unable to observe it without feeling some culpability in these continued acts of violence that have been carried out in our name by our elected leaders.

If we don't express opposition to these crimes, we too are maimed…

World refugee population: 11.5 million
Refugees International, 2008[5]

In Search Of, 2003
Acrylic & Oil Painting

Stripped of roots and links, reality becomes a kingdom of count and discount, where price determines the value of things, of people, and countries. The ones who count arouse desire and envy among those of us the market discounts, in a world where respect is measured by the number of credit cards you carry. The ideologues of fog, the pontificators of the obscurantism now in fashion, tells us reality can't be deciphered, which really means reality can't be changed.

GLOBALIZATION REDUCES INTERNATIONAL
RELATIONS TO A SERIES OF HUMILIATIONS...[6]
Eduardo Galeano

Globalization, 2005
Acrylic Painting

Stripped of roots and links, reality becomes a kingdom of count and discounts, where price determines the value of things, of people, and countries. The ones who count arouse desire and envy among those of us the market discounts, in a world where respect is measured by the number of credit cards you carry. The ideologue of fogs the pontificator... in fashion, tell us reality can't be... means reality can't... of the obscurantism now deciphered, which really be changed.

GLOBALIZATION REDUCES INTERNATIONAL RELATIONS TO A SERIES OF HUMILIATIONS...

GLOBAL

On behalf of relatives on my mother's side -- Ashkenazi Jews who fled their homeland of Austria during Hitler's Anschluss -- it is for them that we say, "Never again."

I speak on behalf of relatives on my father's side who are not living, but dying, under the occupation of this administration's deadly foray in Iraq. From the lack of security, to the lack of basic supplies, to the lack of electricity, to the lack of potable water, to the lack of jobs, to the lack of reconstruction, to the lack of education, to the lack of healthcare, to the lack of life, liberty, and the pursuit of happiness, they are much worse off now than before we invaded.

"Never again" should apply to them, too.[7]

Dr. Dahlia Wasfi

Despair, 2005
Acrylic Painting

For every cluster bomb dropped, a small percentage of the bomblets released are duds. Bright yellow, with red stripes and a little plastic parachute hood, these soda-can-sized death sticks have proven particularly attractive to curious children. Many [youngsters] are blown to bits and killed in the encounter, while others survive despite the loss of limbs.[8]

The Rage Next Time #1, 2006
Acrylic, Pencil Collage

THE
Rag
Next
Time

"I'm getting very upset seeing little kids getting shot," says 9-year-old Yara, a fourth grader at an Orthodox Christian school in Jordan. "From the bottom of my heart I hope [the Iraqis] win this war, and we should help them." How does she feel about Americans? "It's not fair for them to come to another country to take its riches. They just want to frighten people with their might, so the say 'we support you' and they

We are not fighting Al Qaeda in Iraq; we are slaughtering people's children. We went in to liberate Iraqis from a ruthless dictator we imposed upon them who allegedly killed 300,000 during his 30 year reign of terror. We've accomplished more than triple that in a fraction of the time.[9]

The Rage Next Time #2, 2006
Acrylic & Oil Painting

Immigrants have become especially vulnerable to abuse and violence. Whether they are documented or undocumented, immigrants are now the almost exclusive scapegoat for the faltering economy, the threat of terrorism, the deterioration of services, and the social problems afflicting the United States. In this officially condoned anti-immigrant climate, racial profiling, exploitation in the workplace, hate, violence, and multiple public policies are being used to deliberately force immigrants to leave or exist in the shadows.[10]

Fugitives in Their Own Land, 2004
Acrylic & Oil Painting

...Whereas recognition of the inherent dignity and of the equal and

inalienable rights of all members of the human family is the

foundation of freedom, justice and peace in the world...[11]

Preamble from the Universal Declaration of Human Rights, adopted and proclaimed by
the United Nations General Assembly, December 10, 1948

We Serve the World, 2003
Acrylic & Oil Painting

The United States government's insistence on framing issues of migration, as law enforcement and national security matters, has prevented acknowledging and addressing the negative displacement impacts and involuntary migration of workers caused by economic restructuring, particularly the North American Free Trade Agreement (NAFTA). As long as the root causes of migration are denied and ignored, the United States will continue to block economically sustainable development for communities in sending countries, which would ameliorate and eventually decrease migration.[12]

A Portrait of Poverty, 2001
Silkscreen

GLOBALIZATION

A PORTRAIT & POVERTY

A noble task, that of heralding the world of the just and the free; a noble function, that of rejecting a system of hunger and of cages – visible and invisible. But how many yards to the border? How long will those in power continue to give us permission?[13]

Eduardo Galeano

A Noble Task, 2004
Silkscreen

A noble task, that of heralding the world of the just and the free; a noble function, that of rejecting a system of hunger and of cages ~ visible and invisible. But how many yards to the border? How long will those in power continue to give us their permission? Eduardo Galeano

Globalization turns workers into a commodity which can be bought anywhere in the world for the lowest price. They are more than a commodity; they are human beings who demand to be treated with dignity.[14]

Hombre Sin País, 2005
(Man Without a Country)
Lithograph

Abu Ghraib

In the era of Saddam Hussein, Abu Ghraib, twenty miles west of Baghdad, was one of the world's most notorious prisons, with torture, weekly executions, and vile living conditions.[15]

In the same year of the regime's collapse and after a complete renovation, it became a U.S. military prison. Soon after, reports of torture, "systematic and illegal abuse of detainees,"[16] along with very disturbing photographs revealing more details of prisoner abuse, leaked out to the public and exposed the horrific conditions and human rights violations.

U.S. Major General Antonio M. Taguba in his 53 page report, concluded that "institutional failures of the Army prison system were devastating." Specifically, Taguba found that between October and December of 2003 there were numerous instances of "sadistic, blatant, and wanton criminal abuses" at Abu Ghraib perpetrated by soldiers of the 372nd Military Police Company, and also by members of the American intelligence community.[17]

Spreading Democracy...Abou Ghraib, 2005
Oil, Pencil & Silkscreen

Under international law, torture cannot be authorized, condoned or carried out by anyone anywhere. Any government official, employee or contractor who violates this principle – whether lawyer or politician or soldier or interrogator – must be investigated, and where there is evidence of criminal wrongdoing, prosecuted.[18]

Spreading Democracy...Abou Ghraib,
2005
Silkscreen

spreading democracy... abou ghraib

w/c 2   2005

tor.ture (tor'cher) n., v., tured, -tur~ing —n.

1. The act of inflicting excruciating pain, as punishment or revenge, as a means of getting a confession or information, or for shear cruelty.[19]

...Spreading Democracy

Torture...Spreading Democracy, 2005
Silkscreen

tor·ture (tôr′cher), n., v., -tured, -tur·ing. **–n. 1.** The act of inflicting excruciating pain, as punishment or revenge, as a means of getting a confession or information, or for sheer cruelty.

...Spreading Democracy

We do not torture.

We soften them up for interrogation.

Your confessions are ready for you to sign...

Your Confessions are Ready, 2006
Oil Painting

"Your confessions are ready for You to sign"

'06 Malaquías Montoya

You Do Not Know War

By Shereen Hamadeh
Folsom High School, Folsom, California

You do not know war until you stare at the innocence of a charred three-year-old, until you endure the shrills of her wailing mother, until you're burned by the tears of her father and strangled by his agony. You do not know war until you see the elderly asleep beside the corpse of their grandchildren praying atop the rubble of what was once their home, until you're forced to walk a child across her parents' carcasses and try to answer "Why?" The continuous raping of the innocent only impregnates the land with the suicide bomber: the father who finally found cause to hate, the mother whose only slumber must be accompanied by death, by the promising nature of vengeance. They are the government's own illegitimate child, their own product. You tell me that they are terrorists, I agree. Yet I ask you to define the terms, to eliminate the Muslim prerequisite. For is not a terrorist a murderer, one that slaughters inclusively with no regard to military status, race, sex, or age, one that kills with no cause but to destroy freedom? Yet, ask them, go deep into the soul of your so-called terrorist and find the human that yearns, the cause that triggers, the anger that destructs. These so called terrorists are multiplying. With one head down twenty emerge: his brothers, sisters, cousins, and friends, the ones, once neutral, now victims, victims to the murderer, the one who slaughtered with no regard to military status, race, sex, or age, the one who had imprisoned them in bomb shelters and dissolved their freedom, and from there the product evolves, making our once noble cause a foolish cause.

For our justified violence mirrors their justified hate. It's better to fight on their terrain in between their homes and memories and history and sacrifice a couple of their fathers, brothers and children to keep them from coming on our territory. And thus they fight for the freedom of their land and sacrifice a couple of our fathers, brothers and children to keep from losing the little they have. And each side justifies murder with the certainty that one man's blood is more precious than another's. You may bomb the world to pieces but not to peace. There is little rationalization of hate and war and little answer to the young children's questions. There is no manner to erase the trauma in their souls, the trauma that evolves into hate, the hate that continues war, the war that prolongs the cycle; the never-ending pinwheel we refuse to stop spinning.

The end of war comes with the beginning of consciousness, the consciousness of the human race as a single entity. We must stand together human to human, not with our weapons, but with our souls in order to achieve the one almighty goal of peace and harmony. For then, only then, may we all be blessed enough to not know war.[20]

Those Who Lead Children to War,
2007
Acrylic Painting & Pencil

Following 9/11, immigration was tied to terrorism, and in the years that followed, the country has seen a continual deterioration of civil rights. In early 2006, Congress reauthorized the USA PATRIOT Act, legislation passed shortly after 9/11 that gave the Executive Branch sweeping powers to wire tap, search, and jail citizens and non-citizens without probable cause.[21]

America's Descent Toward Fascism, 2007
Acrylic, Pencil, Silkscreen & Collage

AMRICAS
DESCENT
TOWARDS
CIS

Consider the mass demonstrations of spring 2003 when millions took to the streets of Washington, London and San Francisco demanding that there be no war in Iraq. Here in the alleged democracies of England and the United States, governments ignored the people and engaged in an imperial war based on a lie...

We don't live in a democracy we live under the rule of a few.[22]

Mumia Abu-Jamal

Enforcing Democracy, 2007
Charcoal & Silkscreen

Shakir, whose gaunt cheeks are covered by a thin beard, said U.S. interrogators used his relationship with his brother to try to extract a confession. On three occasions following extended sessions, he said, they were taken in Humvees into the desert north of the port. There, he said, they were buried up to their necks in the sand. "I couldn't see my brother," he said. "Then I heard shots fired. They came back and told me my brother was dead."[23]

Scott Wilson

Those Who Refuse #1, 2007
Charcoal & Silkscreen

Captives are often "softened up" by MPs and U.S. Army Special
Forces troops who beat them and confine them in tiny rooms.
The alleged terrorists are commonly blindfolded and thrown into
walls, bound in painful positions, subjected to loud noises, and
deprived of sleep. The tone of intimidation and fear is the beginning, they said, of a process of piercing a prisoner's resistance.
The take-down teams often "package" prisoners for transport, fit-
ting them with hoods and gags, and binding them to stretchers
with duct tape.[24]

Those Who Refuse #2, 2007
Charcoal & Silkscreen

Overleaf:
Those Who Refuse #3, 2007
Charcoal & Silkscreen

Those Who Refuse #4, 2007
Charcoal & Silkscreen

GUANTÁNAMO

Hundreds of people remain detained in Guantánamo, [the U.S.-operated military prison in Cuba] without charge and with little hope of a fair trial. Despite international outrage and the U.S. authorities' own stated wish to close the camp, Guantánamo is still holding detainees illegally. Hundreds languish in cruel, inhuman and degrading conditions, including detainees who have been cleared for release. Detainees continue to be transferred to the camp from secret CIA custody and elsewhere, confirming Guantánamo's role at the heart of the U.S. network of unlawful detention. Guantánamo is a symbol of injustice and abuse.[25]

Guantánamo Bound, 2007
Charcoal

Overleaf:
Untitled, 2006
Charcoal & Colored Pencil

Exhibition Tour

The exhibition tour will continue during the next several years. Contact Lezlie Salkowitz-Montoya: 707.447.4194 or lsmontoya@ earthlink.net regarding new bookings, tour schedules and new venues.

Works in the Exhibition

In Search Of, 2003
Acrylic & Oil Painting, 84" x 60"

Globalization, 2005
Acrylic Painting, 64" x 52"

Despair, 2005
Acrylic Painting, 50" x 48"

The Rage Next Time #1, 2006
Acrylic, Pencil Collage, 30" x 22"

The Rage Next Time #2, 2006
Oil Painting, 65" x 49"

Fugitives in Their Own Land, 2004
Acrylic & Oil Painting, 65" x 49"

We Serve the World, 2003
Acrylic & Oil Painting, 54" x 35"

A Portrait of Poverty, 2001
Silkscreen, 27" x 18"

A Noble Task, 2004
Silkscreen, 30" x 22"

Hombre Sin País, 2005
Man Without a Country
Lithograph, 30" x 22"
Printed at the University of Texas, San Antonio

Spreading Democracy...Abou Ghraib, 2005
Oil, Pencil & Silkscreen, 31" x 25"

Spreading Democracy...Abou Ghraib, 2005
Silkscreen, 30" x 22"
Printed at Coronado Studies, Austin, TX

Torture...Spreading Democracy, 2005
Silkscreen, 30" x 22"

Your Confessions are Ready, 2006
Oil Painting, 47" x 60"

Those Who Lead Children to War, 2007
Acrylic Painting & Pencil, 30" x 22"

America's Descent Toward Fascism, 2007
Acrylic, Pencil, Silkscreen & Collage, 40" x 32"

Enforcing Democracy, 2007
Charcoal & Silkscreen, 30" x 22"

Those Who Refuse #1, 2007
Charcoal & Silkscreen, 30" x 22"

Those Who Refuse #2, 2007
Charcoal & Silkscreen, 30" x 22"

Those Who Refuse #3, 2007
Charcoal & Silkscreen, 30" x 22"

Those Who Refuse #4, 2007
Charcoal & Silkscreen, 30" x 22"

Guantanamo Bound, 2007
Charcoal, 30" x 22"

Untitled, 2006
Charcoal & Colored Pencil, 30" x 22"

Malaquias Montoya

Malaquias Montoya was born in Albuquerque, New Mexico and raised in the San Joaquin Valley of California. He was brought up in a family of seven children by parents who could not read or write either Spanish or English. The three oldest children never went beyond a seventh grade education since the entire family had to work as farm laborers for their survival. His father and mother were divorced when he was ten, and his mother continued to work in the fields to support the four children still remaining at home so they could pursue their education. Montoya graduated with honors from the University of California, Berkeley in 1969.

Montoya has lectured and taught at numerous colleges and universities in the San Francisco Bay Area including Stanford, the University of California, Berkeley, and the California College of Arts and Crafts in Oakland. He has also served as Director of the Taller de Artes Graficas, in East Oakland, where he produced various prints and conducted many community art workshops. Since 1989 Montoya has been a professor at the University of California, Davis, teaching both in the Department of Art and the Department of Chicana/o Studies. In 2000, Montoya spent a semester as Visiting Professor in the Art Department at the University of Notre Dame, in Indiana, and he continues to work collaboratively with the Institute for Latino Studies at Notre Dame. Montoya's classes include silkscreening, poster making, and mural painting, with a focus on Chicano culture and history. His own works include acrylic paintings, murals, washes, and drawings, but he is primarily known for his silkscreen prints, which have been exhibited nationally as well as internationally. Montoya is credited by historians as one of the founders of the social serigraphy movement in the San Francisco Bay Area in the mid-1960's.

Montoya's unique visual expression is an art of protest, depicting the strength of humanity in the face of injustice and the necessity to unite behind that struggle. Montoya's artistic philosophy guides his work and his life. Although he addresses many issues, the three prominent themes that run through his work are injustice, empowerment and international struggle. He celebrates small and large victories of the human spirit, depicting people working together to change and transform their lives. Montoya's images serve as a bridge between struggles, helping us better understand the world in which we live and demonstrating that those who live on the margins must unite against common antagonists – the crippling forces of cultural and political imperialism. His work bears the imprint of Chicano Art, however, it reaches far beyond the Chicano community and speaks to the disenfranchised across continents.

Lezlie Salkowitz-Montoya
Elmira, CA

References and Notes

1. Adolfo Pérez Esquivel, Acceptance Speech, on the occasion of the award of the Nobel Peace Prize in Oslo, December 10, 1980, From <u>Nobel Lectures</u>, *Peace 1971-1980*, (Singapore: World Scientific Publishing Co., Editor-in-Charge Tore Frängsmyr, Editor Irwin Abrams, 1997)
   http://nobelprize.org/nobel_prizes/peace/laureates/1980/esquivel-acceptance-sp.html

2. Ibid.
   http://nobelprize.org/nobel_prizes/peace/laureates/1980/esquivel-acceptance.html

3. Malaquias Montoya & Lezlie Salkowitz-Montoya, *PreMeditated: Meditations on Capital Punishment, Works by Malaquias Montoya,* (Elmira, CA & Notre Dame, IN: Co-published by Malaquias Montoya & Lezlie Salkowitz-Montoya, and the Institute for Latino Studies, University of Notre Dame).
   http://www.malaquiasmontoya.com/ http://www.malaquiasmontoya.com/Catalogue_Montoya.pdf

4. Smedley D. Butler, *War is a Racket,* (NY, New York: Round Table Press, Inc., 1935), pp. 1--2.

5. Refugees International, A Powerful Voice for Lifesaving Action, 2001 S Street NW, Suite 700, Washington, DC 20009.

   Refugees International generates lifesaving humanitarian assistance and protection for displaced people around the world, and works to end the conditions that create displacement.
   http://www.refintl.org/

6. Eduardo Galeano, *Upside Down, A PRIMER FOR THE LOOKING-GLASS WORLD*, (New York: Metropolitan Books, Henry Holt and Company, LLC, 2000), p. 308.

7. Dahlia Wasfi, M.D., "The Legacy of Oppression and The Legitimacy of Resistance." Testimony from the Democratic Congressional Forum on Iraq, April 27, 2006
   http://www.liberatethis.com/index.html

   Dr. Dahlia Wasfi spent her early childhood in Saddam Hussein's Iraq until she returned with her family to the United States in 1977. She graduated from Swarthmore College in 1993 with a B.A. in Biology, and in 1997 graduated from the University of Pennsylvania School of Medicine. After years of separation, Wasfi visited Iraq to see her family in Basrah and Baghdad. Based on her experiences, she is speaking out against the negative effect of the U.S. invasion on the Iraqi people and the need to end the occupation.
   http://www.globalexchange.org/getInvolved/speakers/124.html

8. Jeffrey Benner, "The Case Against Cluster Bombs," *Mother Jones Magazine,* May, 28, 1999.
   http://www.motherjones.com/news/special_reports/total_coverage/kosovo/reality_check/cluster.html

9. Dr. Dahlia Wasfi, op.cit.

10. *Over-Raided, Under Siege, U.S. Immigration Laws and Enforcement Destroy the Rights of Immigrants.* A report on human rights violations perpetrated against immigrant and refugee families, workers and communities in the U.S., 2008. Human Rights Immigrant Community Action Network; an initiative of the National Network for Immigrant and Refugee Rights, pp. v,vi.

    Over-Raided, Under Siege, U.S. Immigration Laws and Enforcement Destroy the Rights of Immigrants is written annually to report human rights violations perpetrated against immigrant and refugee families, workers and communities in the U.S.
    http://www.nnirr.org/resources/docs/UnderSiege_web.pdf

11. *Universal Declaration of Human Rights*, adopted and proclaimed by the United Nations General Assembly resolution 217 A (III). December 10, 1948, Preamble.
    http://www.state.gov/g/drl/rls/60372.htm

12. *Over-Raided, Under Siege, U.S. Immigration Laws and Enforcement Destroy the Rights of Immigrants.* op.cit. p. 47.

13. Eduardo Galeano, *Days and Nights of Love and War,* (London: Pluto Press, 2000), p. 170.

14. Vicky Funari & Sergio De La Torre, Producers/Directors, *Maquilapolis; [city of factories],* (South Burlington, VT: California Newsreel/Resolution, 2006).

15. Seymour M. Hersh, "Torture at Abu Ghraib, American soldiers brutalized Iraqis. How far up does the responsibility go?" *The New Yorker,* May 10, 2004.

16. Maj. Gen. Antonio M. Taguba, *U.S. Army Report on Iraqi Prisoner Abuse*, Executive summary of Article 15-6 investigation of the 800th Military Police Brigade. NBC News, Tues., May. 4, 2004
   http://www.msnbc.msn.com/id/4894001/

17. Ibid.

18. Amnesty International USA, "Impunity and injustice in the 'war on terror' From torture in secret detention to execution after unfair trial?" February 2008, AI Index: AMR 51/012/2008, p. 3.
   http://www.amnesty.org/en/library/info/AMR51/012/2008/en

19. *The Random House Dictionary of the English Language,* (New York: Random House, 1966), p.1497.

20. Shereen Hamadeh, "You Do Not Know War." High School Scholarship Essay Contest, *Physicians for Social Responsibility*, Sacramento Chapter, 2007
   http://www.sacpsr.org/default.htm

21. *Over-Raided, Under Siege, U.S. Immigration Laws and Enforcement Destroy the Rights of Immigrants*. op.cit. p. 53.
   http://www.nnirr.org/resources/docs/UnderSiege_web.pdf

22. Mumia Abu-Jamal, "When Democracy Equals Empire," Prison Radio, March 7, 2004
   http://www.prisonradio.org/maj/maj_3_7_04empire.html

   Mumia Abu-Jamal is a renowned journalist from Philadelphia who has been in prison since 1981 and on death row since 1983 for allegedly shooting Philadelphia police officer Daniel Faulkner. He is known as the "Voice of the Voiceless" for his award-winning reporting on police brutality and other social and racial epidemics that plague communities of color in Philadelphia and throughout the world. His case is currently on appeal before the Federal District Court in Philadelphia. Mumia's fight for a new trial has won the support of tens of thousands around the world.
   http://www.freemumia.org/

23. Scott Wilson, "Angry Ex-Detainees Tell of Abuse, Iraqis Say They Endured Physical, Psychological Hardship in U.S. Custody," *Washington Post,* Foreign Service, Monday, May 3, 2004, p. A01.
   http://www.washingtonpost.com/ac2/wp-dyn/A61560-2004May2?language=printer

24. Dana Priest & Barton Gellman, "U.S. Decries Abuse but Defends Interrogations 'Stress and Duress' Tactics Used on Terrorism Suspects Held in Secret Overseas Facilities," *Washington Post,* Staff Writers, Thursday, December 26, 2002. p. A01.
   http://www.washingtonpost.com/ac2/wp-dyn?pagename=article&contentId=A37943-2002Dec25

25. Amnesty International, "CLOSE GUANTÁNAMO," COUNTER TERROR WITH JUSTICE, Issues.
   http://www.amnesty.org/en/campaigns/counter-terror-with-justice/issues/close-guantanamo

An electronic version of this catalogue, with live links, can be viewed online at www.malaquiasmontoya.com

A portion of the proceeds from the sale of this catalogue will go to the following national organizations working on human rights issues on an international basis.

AMNESTY INTERNATIONAL

Amnesty International's vision is of a world in which every person enjoys all of the human rights enshrined in the Universal Declaration of Human Rights and other international human rights standards. In pursuit of this vision, AI's mission is to undertake research and action focused on preventing and ending grave abuses of the rights to physical and mental integrity, freedom of conscience and expression, and freedom from discrimination, within the context of its work to promote all human rights. Amnesty International is independent of any government, political ideology, economic interest or religion. It does not support or oppose any government or political system, nor does it support or oppose the views of the victims whose rights it seeks to protect. It is concerned solely with the impartial protection of human rights.

Amnesty International
5 Penn Plaza # 16
New York, NY 10001
http://www.amnestyusa.org

THE VALENTINO ACHAK DENG FOUNDATION believes that the strength, determination, and diversity of the Sudanese people will enable them to build a peaceful and prosperous future. Their aim is to empower war-affected Sudanese populations by seeking to improve U.S. Policy toward Sudan by educating the public and policy makers on the situation in Sudan. They work to rebuild southern Sudanese communities through the implementation of community-driven development projects that increase access to educational opportunities for children, women, and men. The Valentino Achak Deng Foundation also helps provide scholarships to aid the educational pursuits of Sudanese-Americans by supporting community organizations and educational institutions that work with members of the Sudanese Diaspora.

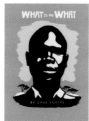

What Is the What

Dave Eggers's *What Is the What* is the novelized autobiography of Valentino Achak Deng, from his pre-war life in southern Sudan to his resettlement in the United States. All proceeds from the book go to aiding the Sudanese in America and Sudan.

The Valentino Achak Deng Foundation
849 Valencia Street
San Francisco, CA 94110
http://www.valentinoachakdeng.org

NATIONAL LABOR COMMITTEE helps to defend the human rights of workers in the global economy. The NLC investigates and exposes human and labor rights abuses committed by U.S. companies producing goods in the developing world. They undertake public education, research and popular campaigns that empower U.S. citizens to support the efforts of workers to learn and defend their rights. As they fight for the right to work in dignity, in healthy and safe workplaces and to earn a living wage, the NLC will work with them to provide international visibility and backing for their efforts--and to press for international legal frameworks with effective enforcement mechanisms that will help create a space where fundamental internationally recognized worker rights can be assured.

National Labor Committee
75 Varick Street, Suite 1500
New York, NY 10013
http://www.nlcnet.org